bicycle tra

with illustrations by n

D0924703

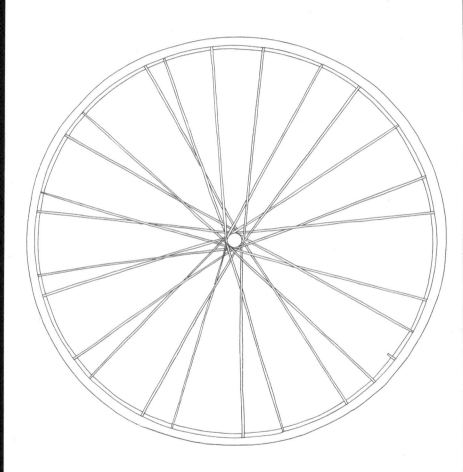

ISBN 13: 978-1-85669-900-6

this travel journal belongs to:

if lost please contact:

in case of an emergency please call:

journal started on:

location:

useful information:

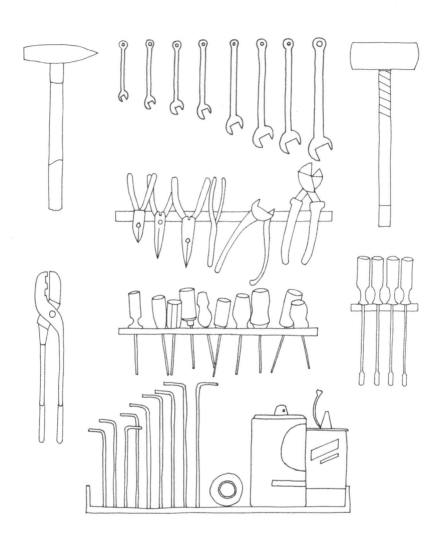

tools

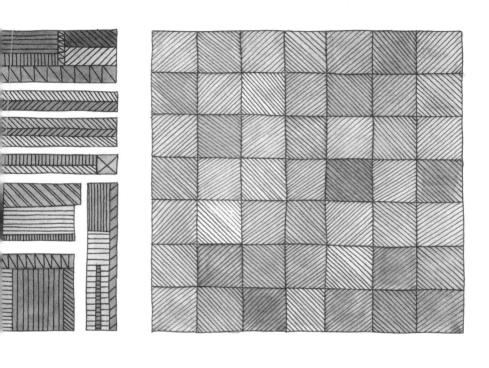

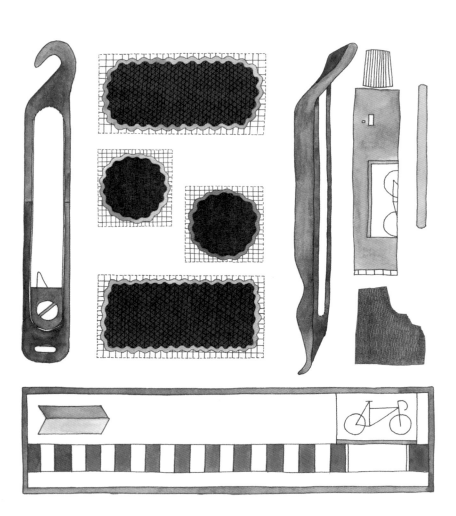

puncture repair kit

punctures
front wheel
time/location

punctures
rear wheel
time/location

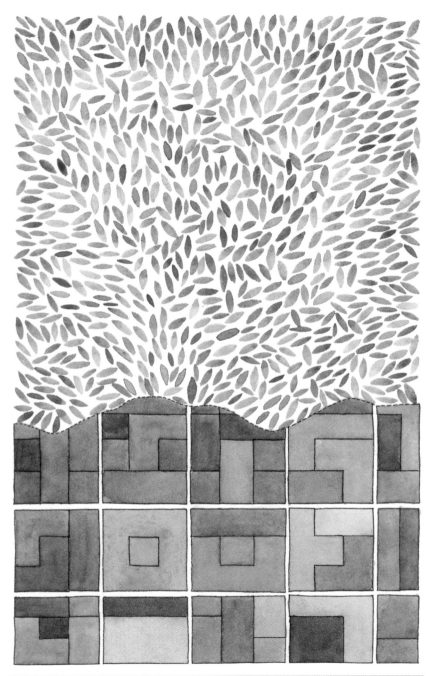

where city meets nature

bridges and river

bike ropes

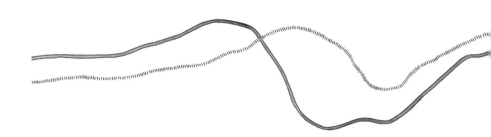

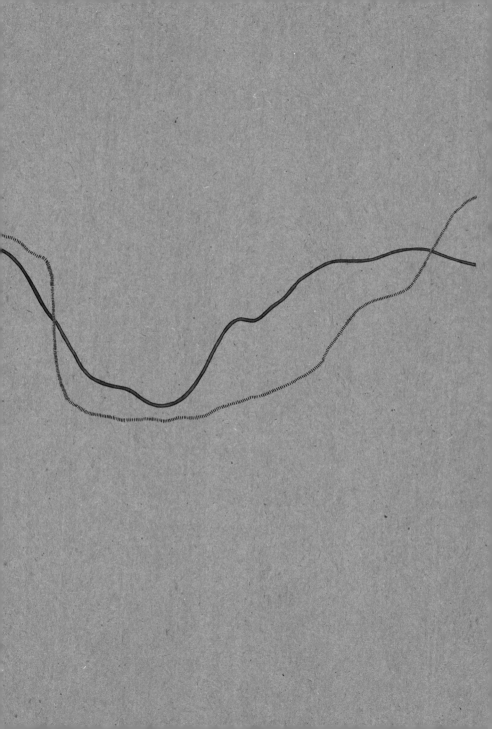

forest

lake by forest

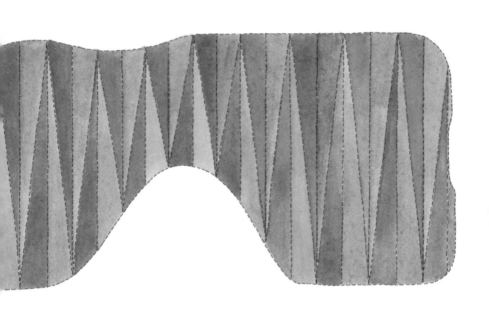

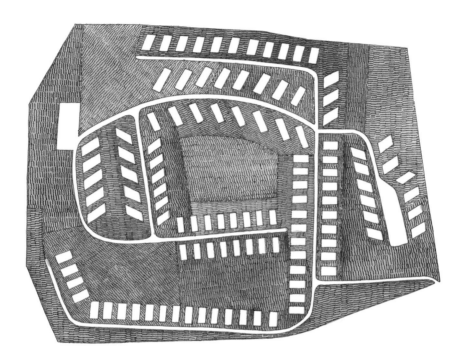

caravan park

mountains

altitude

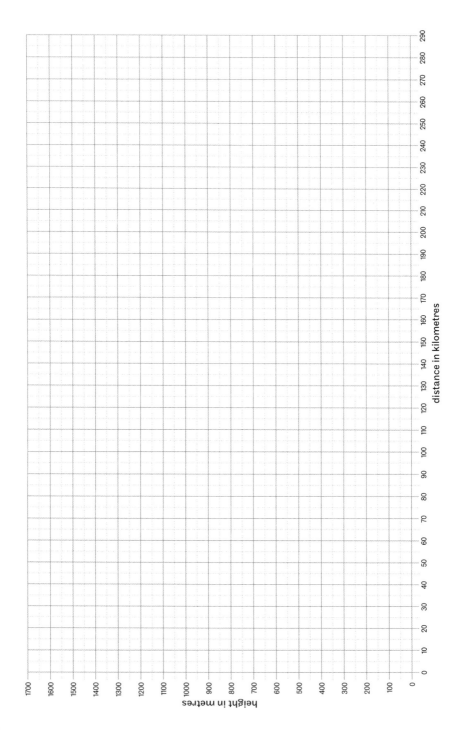

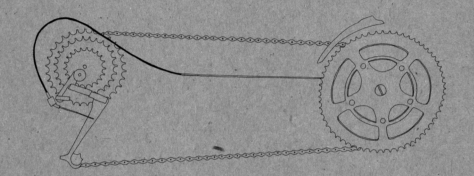

chain-gears

altitude

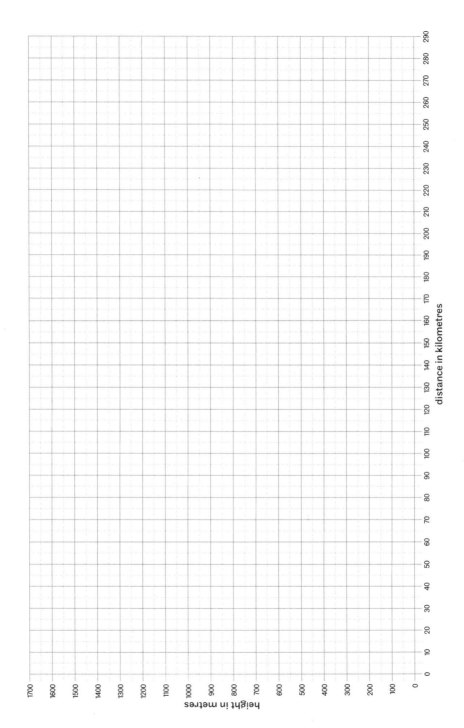

uphill and downhill

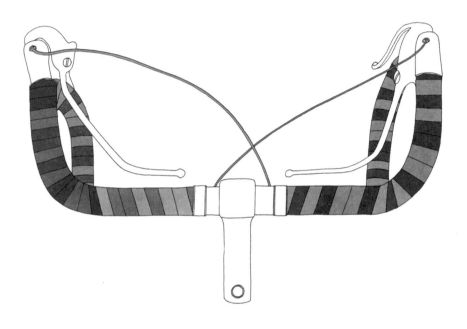

handlebars

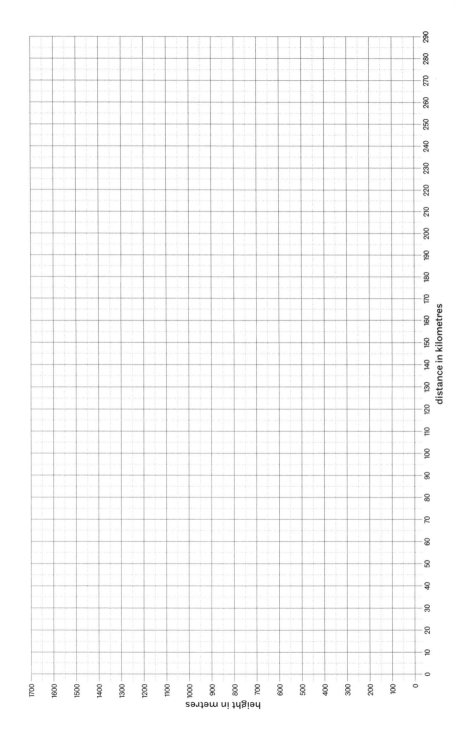

horizon line

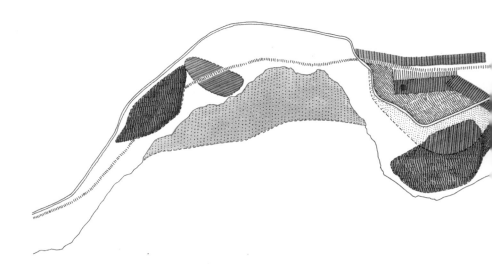

route along the coast

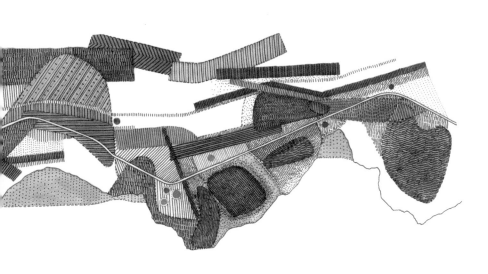

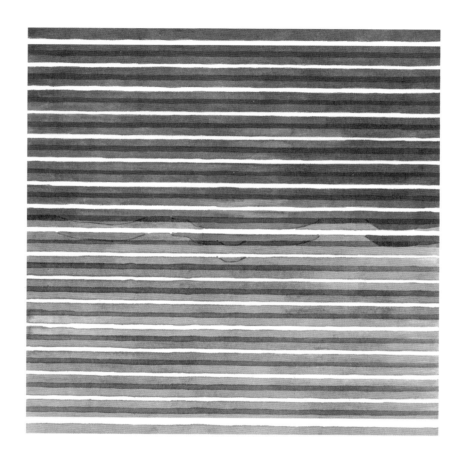

where the land meets sea